Paper Punching

Dedicated to
Alice Martha Morgan and
Liam Anderson Morgan

Paper Punching

Michelle Powell

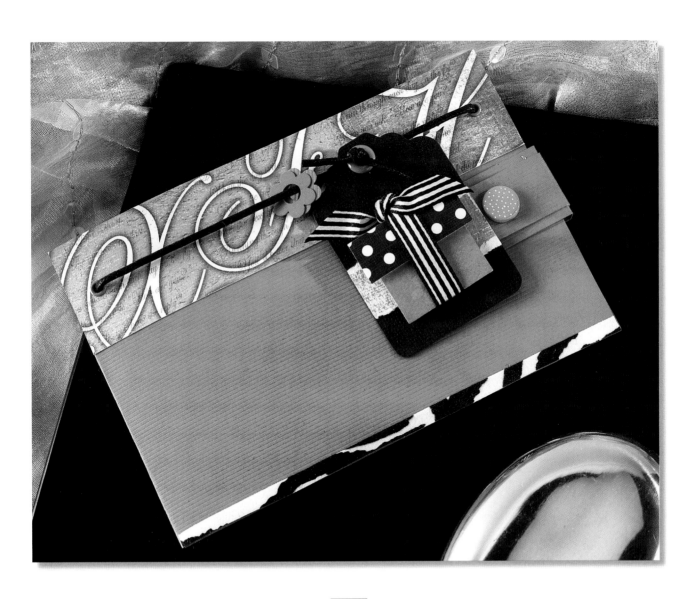

SEARCH PRESS

First published in Great Britain 2007

Search Press Limited
Wellwood, North Farm Road,
Tunbridge Wells, Kent TN2 3DR

Text copyright © Michelle Powell 2007

Photographs by Debbie Patterson at Search Press studios and by Roddy Paine Photographic Studios

Photographs and design copyright © Search Press Ltd 2007

ISBN-13: 978-1-84448-167-5

The Publishers and author can accept no responsibility for any consequences arising from the information, advice or instructions given in this publication.

Readers are permitted to reproduce any of the items in this book for their personal use, or for the purposes of selling for charity, free of charge and without the prior permission of the Publishers. Any use of the items for commercial purposes is not permitted without the prior permission of the Publishers.

Suppliers

If you have difficulty in obtaining any of the materials and equipment mentioned in this book, then please visit the Search Press website for details of suppliers: www.searchpress.com

---

Publisher's note

All the step-by-step photographs in this book feature the author, Michelle Powell, demonstrating the craft of paper punching. No models have been used.

Acknowledgements

Many thanks as always go to the team at Search Press, to Roz Dace for believing in me, to Edd Ralph for his hard work and humour, to Debbie Patterson for making the photography such fun and producing beautiful photos, and to Ellie Burgess for her design skills.

Huge thanks go to Mum and Dad who remain focussed and jolly thoughout my most stressed moments and happily do anything and everything they can to help.

Thanks go to Duane for at least giving craft punching a try – your flower was beautiful.

Last (but never least) to Christian for feeding me while I cut, punched, folded and glued, for putting our social life on hold to help out and for tolerating attending work randomly splattered with pink glitter!

Page 1: Flower Pot
Decorate a paint tin with an oversized and colourful punched flower to create an unusual gift box.

Page 3: Pink Gift Wallet
Use simple square, tag and circle punches to create this funky gift voucher wallet.

Opposite: Wedding Candle
Decorate a glass tealight holder using punched shapes and coordinated paper.

Contents

Introduction

Craft punches are essentially variations on the traditional hole punch with shaped holes rather than just circles. I bought my first punches – a small star, a heart and a teddy bear – in America about fifteen years ago. As a keen papercrafter, I was delighted to find these new crafting tools and used them to decorate cards and envelopes. The idea back then was to use the hole as the decorative element and throw away the punched shape. As a passionate hoarder, I soon started using the punched shapes, creating flowers from hearts and cutting down my stars to create party hats for teddy!

Over the last ten or so years punches have evolved to become larger and more intricate, and they are now available in hundreds of different types and designs, including beautiful flower shapes, animals and objects, basic shapes, borders and corner decorators – even mini envelopes, ready to fold.

When you first punch a design, do not be disheartened. A plain shape can look rather uninspiring, but the key skill in working with punches is knowing how to transform that dull, flat shape into something beautiful. This book will show you how to fold, shape, combine, chalk, glitter and embellish your punched designs to really bring them to life and create professional-quality paper projects.

The techniques in this book are suitable for all. If you are new to punching, you will be amazed at just how quick and easy it is to create beautiful effects with punched shapes. For the more experienced, this book will inspire you to get so much more from your punches with several great new ways of using them such as punching glitter stickers, creating three-dimensional punched flowers and folding punched shapes to make amazing medallion effects.

Whether your passion is for cardmaking, giftmaking, scrapbooking or paper crafts, this book is sure to inspire you to reach for that long-forgotten punch and have a go.

Happy punching!

Michelle

Materials

All of the projects featured in this book use materials that are readily available in any high street craft store. The great beauty of paper punching is that you only need your punch and some paper to get started. Even recycled papers, junk mail or leftover scraps from other projects are ideal to use with this craft.

Craft punches

Punches come in a huge selection of shapes, sizes and types. Most good craft stores will stock a large selection and even more are available to purchase online. If your budget is limited, go for punches with simple shapes like circles, squares and ovals. They may not look as attractive on the store shelf, but are far more versatile and therefore offer better value for money.

For a basic set consider circles, a single small hole punch, a simple flower shape and a basic tag shape, as these are punches that you will use over and over again. I find that medium and large punches are far more useful than the very small ones.

Most punches are designed so that you use the piece that is punched out, and designs include everything from wedding dresses to lobsters! Some punches, such as the ornate and mosaic types are designed so that you use the negative shape and the punched pieces from these are generally too small to use. These create nice effects but their uses are more limited.

Border punches and **circle punches** cut the edge off your paper and create a pretty perforated design along the edge.

Corner punches cut the corner of your paper into a design, sometimes with embossing or further cut decoration.

Tumble punches are designed so that the punched shape can be folded to create a three-dimensional effect.

Tip

Use your punches to create stencils by punching through some scrap paper, then chalking or inking through the holes. This technique is great for floral backgrounds or adding dotty patterns.

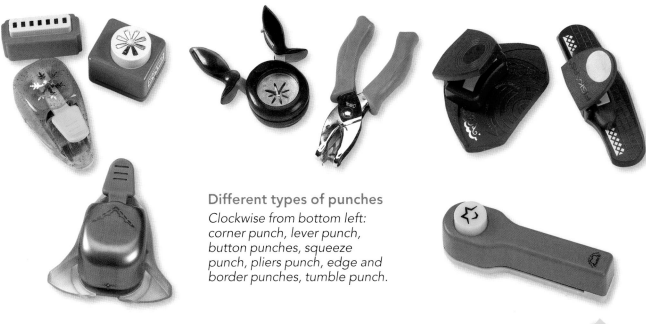

Different types of punches
Clockwise from bottom left: corner punch, lever punch, button punches, squeeze punch, pliers punch, edge and border punches, tumble punch.

Papers and cards

Most types of paper and thin card are suitable to use with punches, but some thicker card will not punch at all. The simple rule is that the more complicated the punch design, the thinner the paper should be. The easy way to find out is to try. Do not force the punch, just apply adequate pressure and if it cuts through cleanly and easily then you know that paper is fine for punching.

Plain coloured papers are the most versatile and the majority of projects in this book simply use plain thin card to achieve a multitude of effects.

Patterned and other unusual papers

Many beautiful patterned papers are available that can really make the difference to your creative work. Smaller patterns are better for use with punches because your punched piece will still show the pattern clearly.

Heavily textured papers or papers with a plastic coating may not punch well, so use these as accents and backgrounds to complement your punched shapes.

Very thin papers may need to be punched between two sheets of plain photocopy paper or glued to a sheet of thin card so that they cut cleanly.

Blanks to decorate

Look out for paint tins, small boxes, mini plant pots and box canvases in high street shops, as these all can be decorated with punched paper.

Tip

Place double-sided tape on the back of your paper before punching to create mini stickers that are ready to attach to your blanks.

Embellishments

Ribbon, craft jewels, wire, brads, eyelets, staples, buttons and beads have all been used in the projects in this book. The smallest embellishment can really add the finishing touch to your creations. Glitter, applied with a glue pen or double-sided tape, has also been used for a touch of sparkle.

Tip

Punch tiny circles of metallic or iridescent card and use them as you would craft jewels – you will hardly notice the difference.

Other items

Pencil Used to draw lines and mark measurements.

Ruler Used to measure and draw straight lines, to create straight cuts and to score lines.

Craft knife and scissors A craft knife is used to cut straight lines with a ruler. Scissors are used to cut out shapes and trim ribbon.

Cutting mat Used with a craft knife to protect your work surface and make cutting easier.

Eyelet setter and hammer Set eyelets into the small punched holes using a setter and hammer.

Chalks with applicator Used to apply softly shaded colour to punched shapes.

Foam stamp and inkpad Stamp background images for your punched designs using a foam stamp and inkpad.

Glue pen Attach fine lines of glitter using a glue pen.

Double-sided tape Use this to assemble most of the project elements.

3D foam pads Used to achieve a three-dimensional effect when layering punched elements.

Clear adhesive Used to glue wire to punched shapes.

Pens Add details to your punched designs with fine line pens.

Scrap paper Used as a base for chalking, stamping and glittering to protect your work surface.

Perforating tool Create decorative lines of perforations that look like mini stitching using a perforating tool.

Scoring tool Use this to score lines to make folding easier and neater.

Fun foam and ball-tipped stylus Use scraps of fun foam with a ball-tipped stylus to shape your punched designs.

Round-nosed pliers and wire cutter Used to cut and shape wire embellishments.

Circle cutter Used to cut circles of paper for covering tin lids.

Air-drying clay Used to weight mini flower pots for the punched flower projects.

Magnets Used as magnetic clasps for handbag-style gift bags and gift wallets.

Glass slides Create shaker boxes using ground-edged glass microscope slides.

Paint and paintbrush Add painted accents to your projects.

Punching paper

Using craft punches

All punches work in essentially the same way: two sharpened metal shapes are engineered to slide together perfectly, acting like scissors to cut or 'punch' the shape from card or paper.

Most punches are button punches, which have a large button on top to press to punch the shape. Sometimes quite a lot of force is needed to use this kind of punch – if this is difficult for you, you can either stand on the punch (wear flat shoes and be careful) or use a punch aid to make the punching easier.

Lever punches are also commonly available. As the name suggests, these punches have a large lever to press. The lever action reduces the force needed, making them easier to use than button punches.

Squeeze punches, which have two handles, are also available. When the handles are squeezed together, the shape is punched out. Again, these use leverage to make the punching easier.

Pliers punches look similar to a pair of pliers and need to be squeezed to cut the shape. These are very easy to use but are only available for smaller, less intricate shapes.

Tip

A punch aid can make using button punches much easier. Place the punch and paper in the punch aid, then press down on the lever to add greater force than when punching by hand.

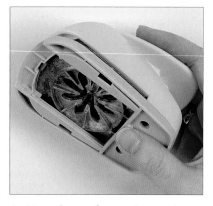

1. Turn the craft punch upside-down, so that you can see the metal punch shape.

Tip

Most punches have a plastic or metal tray for collecting the punched shapes. I always remove this so I can see where I am punching in order to conserve paper.

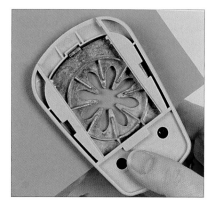

2. Slide the paper into the punch until the paper fills the punch shape.

3. Press the punch to punch out the shape.

Caring for your punches

With a little care your punches should last a lifetime.

Punching through fine sandpaper helps to keep the punch sharp.

If your punch gets sticky, punch through greaseproof paper to clean it.

Using a lubricant pen can also help fix sticky punches. This is especially useful after punching through double-sided tape.

Pliers, button and lever punches were used to make this pot.

Wedding Card

A few simple punched shapes are all that is needed to create an effective card. This project uses a square punch as a backing for use with three differently shaped punches. Together they create a mosaic effect.

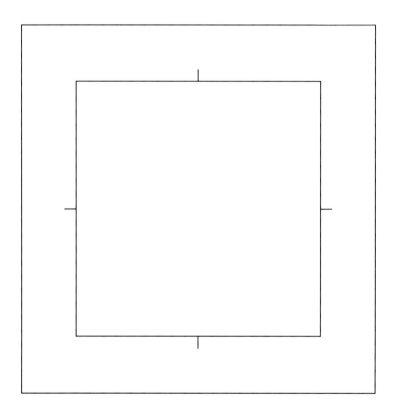

Choose your papers carefully for this project, selecting a colour-coordinated variety of textures and patterns to add interest to the card. This quick and simple card is designed for a wedding invitation, but by varying the shaped punches used, it could be easily adapted for any occasion.

You will need

- Textured purple card 13 x 26cm (5 x 10¼in)

- Craft punches: 2cm (¾in) square, small horseshoe, small heart, small six-petalled flower

- Craft knife, cutting mat and ruler

- 3D foam pads

- Sheets of card: chequered, iridescent, heavily textured, glitter, holographic, matt silver, pink textured, purple foil and metallic purple

- Scrap paper for the template

The template for the Wedding Card, reproduced here at three-quarters of the actual size. You will need to enlarge this by 133 per cent on a photocopier.

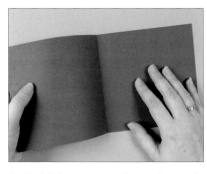

1. Fold the textured purple card in half.

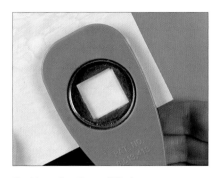

2. Use the 2cm (¾in) square punch to punch a square from the iridescent card.

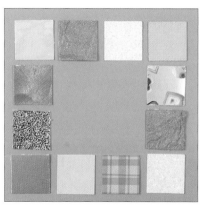

3. Punch eleven more squares from the following pieces of card; clockwise from top left: iridescent, heavily textured, glitter, pink textured, holographic, heavily textured, glitter, chequered, iridescent, matt silver, purple foil and metallic purple. Put these squares to one side.

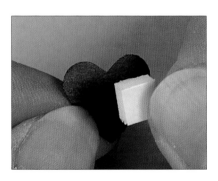

4. Use the heart, horseshoe and six-petalled flower punches to punch out the following shapes; clockwise from top left: textured purple heart (see inset), glitter horseshoe, textured purple flower, holographic heart, heavily-textured horseshoe, glitter flower, purple foil heart, matt silver horseshoe, heavily-textured purple flower, textured pink heart, iridescent horseshoe, chequered flower.

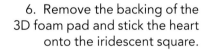

5. Attach a 3D foam pad to the back of the textured purple heart.

6. Remove the backing of the 3D foam pad and stick the heart onto the iridescent square.

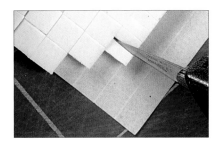

7. Use a craft knife to cut a 3D foam pad in half.

8. Place one half of the foam pad on one side of the back of the glitter horseshoe, and the other on the opposite side.

9. Remove the backing and stick the horseshoe on to the heavily-textured square.

10. Place a 3D foam pad on the back of the textured purple flower, remove the backing and place on the glitter square.

11. Place 3D foam pads on the back of each punched square as shown.

12. Work clockwise around the card shapes and squares, attaching the shapes to the card squares with 3D foam pads, then placing 3D foam pads on the back of each card square.

13. Place the template on the folded purple card, making sure the fold is at the top.

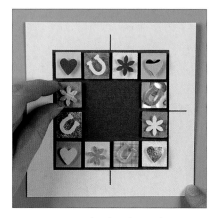

14. Remove the backing from the 3D foam pads and attach each of the squares to the purple card, lining them up within the template.

The finished card.

Opposite
Create a matching tag for a favour bag using the same techniques.

This technique can be adapted to create a full set of matching stationery for a wedding celebration.

Add punched squares and wedding motifs to a glass tealight holder to create a pretty table decoration.

Punch decorations for a tall menu card and order of service sheets.

Create favours for the tables, a cake box, make individual place cards or simply punch your own confetti.

Seasonal Snowman

If you do not have the specific shape of punch you need, try making up the design using a combination of punched shapes. This card uses simple circles and flower shapes to construct a punched snowman. It is amazing just how many different designs you can create by combining punches. Circles are particularly useful for combining, but take a new look at all your punches to see what else they could be used for.

This project also uses small punched pieces as confetti to fill a little shaker box.

You will need

- Craft punches: large circle 2.7cm (1¹⁄₁₆in), medium circle 2.4cm (¹⁵⁄₁₆in), small circle 1.6cm (⅝in), buttonhole pliers, eight-pointed flower, snowflake, flower stamen and small daisy

- Plain white card 21 x 15cm (8¼ x 6in)

- Sheets of card: textured white, double-sided stripy, pale brown, orange, black, turquoise and speckled blue

- Craft jewels, glitter and microbeads

- Two glass slides

- Coloured chalks

- HB pencil

- 3D foam squares and double-sided tape

- Craft knife, cutting mat and ruler

- Clear adhesive

Tip

A buttonhole punch is designed to punch holes to make stitching a button on to paper easy, but it can also be used to create a neat pair of eyes.

1. Fold the white card in half.

2. Use the medium circle punch to punch a circle from textured white card. This will be the snowman's body.

3. Use the buttonhole punch to punch two small holes in the textured white card.

4. Use the small circle punch to punch a circle with the holes just above the centre. This will be the snowman's face.

5. Use the eight-pointed flower punch to punch the shape from striped paper.

6. Use a craft knife to cut the petals shown from the shape. This will form his scarf.

7. Use the flower stamen punch to punch two shapes from pale brown card.

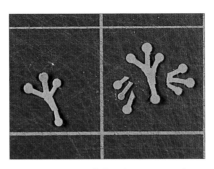

8. Use the craft knife to trim the shapes down as shown. These will be the snowman's arms.

9. Punch a shape from orange card with the daisy punch, then cut one of the petals from the daisy to create the carrot nose.

10. Use a little pink chalk to add colour to the snowman's cheeks, and pencil on a smile.

11. Add a touch of clear adhesive to the back of the flower petal and use the craft knife to place it on the snowman's face as his nose.

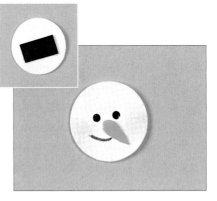

12. Turn his face over and use clear adhesive to stick a small scrap of black paper (see inset) over the holes.

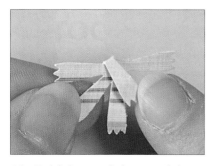

13. Fold the top left part of the scarf over across the centre of the punched shape.

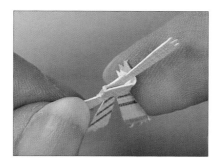

14. Make a crease and fold the piece around the centre. Glue the end of the piece flat on the back.

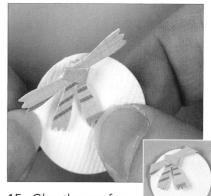

15. Glue the scarf to the snowman's body, then fold the overhanging edges to the back (see inset).

16. Use spots of glue to attach the arms as shown.

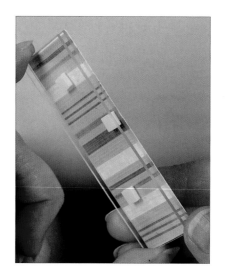

17. Cut a piece of striped card 2.5 x 7.5cm (1 x 3in) and attach it to a glass slide with double-sided tape. Use 3D foam pads to secure a second glass slide to the front of the paper as shown.

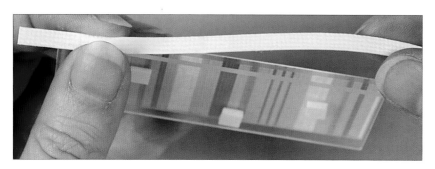

18. Cut a strip of textured white card 0.4 x 21cm (¼ x 8¼in), run double-sided tape on the back, remove the backing and then stick it on the edge of the glass slides to cover the gap between them.

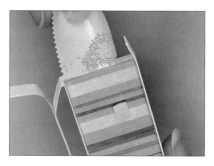

19. When you have covered three sides, tip microbeads and glitter into the top, between the glass slides.

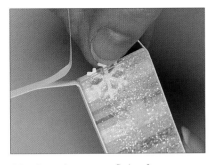

20. Punch a snowflake from white card and put it between the glass slides.

21. Remove the rest of the double-sided tape's backing and close the top by running the card over the gap.

22. Use clear adhesive to stick the piece to the front of the folded white card, then glue the snowman's body on to the front glass slide, covering the lowest 3D foam pad with his body.

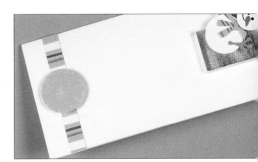

23. Put a 3D foam pad on the back of the snowman's head, remove the backing and place it on top of the body.

24. Punch two snowflakes from white card and place a small craft jewel in the centre of each.

25. Cut a strip of striped paper 7.5 x 1cm (3 x ½in) and stick it to the bottom of the card, then punch a large circle from speckled card and stick it in the centre of the strip using 3D foam pads.

26. Punch a medium circle from turquoise card (see inset), then use the large punch around this smaller hole to punch out a hollow ring.

27. Stick the ring on to the speckled circle at the bottom, then glue one snowflake to the centre. Glue the other snowflake to the glass above the snowman, covering the remaining 3D foam pad visible under the glass slide.

The finished card.

Opposite

Use a cut-down flower and fern frond to make an island palm tree, complete with sea-themed shaker boxes.

Cut down a flower-shaped punch and combine with a stamen punch and mini flower punch to create fun flip-flops for this summery card.

Use circles and heart punches to create colourful fish.

Glitzy Gift Bag

These girly handbags are such a cute way to give a special gift and for once the packing will not immediately be thrown in the bin!

This project uses flower designs to punch double-sided tape so that glitter can be applied. By using further smaller punched flower shapes as masks, you can achieve beautiful colour shading effects with glitter. Special double-sided punch paper is available, but most types will work with punches as long as they are paper rather than plastic based. See the care tips on page 13 for cleaning your punches if they become sticky.

See the care tips on page 13

You will need

- Craft punches: medium hole pliers 3mm (⅛in), flower pliers, medium daisy, small daisy, corner-rounding, large five-petalled flower, large daisy and eight-pointed star
- Craft knife, cutting mat and ruler
- Foam squares and double-sided tape
- Magnets
- Double-sided punch tape
- Ball-tipped stylus
- HB pencil
- Light bronze, dark bronze, green, dark pink and pink glitter
- Perforating tool
- Brads
- Brown card 30 x 30cm (12 x 12in)
- Sheets of card: green, pink and yellow glitter
- Scrap paper for the template
- Glue pen and clear adhesive

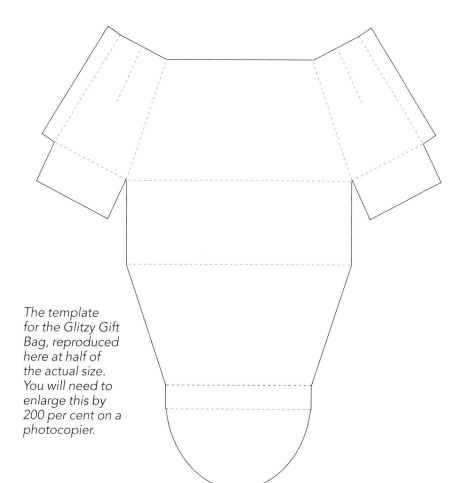

The template for the Glitzy Gift Bag, reproduced here at half of the actual size. You will need to enlarge this by 200 per cent on a photocopier.

Tip

Save the waxy backing paper from your double-sided tape sheets to use as the masks.

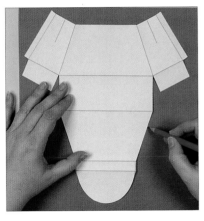

1. Transfer the template to paper, cut it out and then draw round it with a pencil on to brown card.

2. Carefully make marks at the fold lines with the pencil.

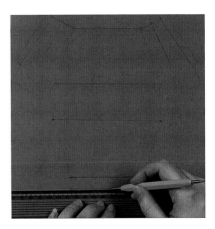

3. Use a ruler and pencil to join the relevant fold lines, referring to the template to make sure; then use a ball-tipped stylus and a ruler to score each fold line.

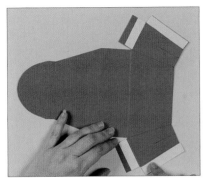

4. Carefully cut out the bag shape with a craft knife, then run double-sided tape along the tabs as shown.

5. Use the medium daisy punch to punch ten daisies from double-sided punch tape.

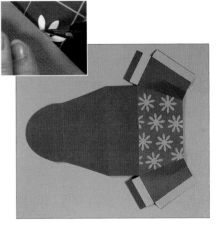

6. Place the daisies on the bag shape as shown. Trim off any that overlap the edges of the bag, folding other parts underneath if necessary (see inset).

7. Use the small daisy punch to punch ten daisies from some scrap backing paper.

8. Remove the backing from the medium daisies and place the small daisies in the centres to act as a mask.

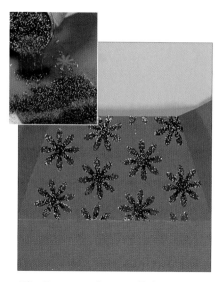

9. Sprinkle the daisies with light bronze glitter.

10. Remove the small daisy masks and sprinkle the daisy centres with dark bronze glitter.

11. Cut a strip of brown card 15 x 0.5cm (6 x ¼in). Run the perforating tool along both edges of the strip.

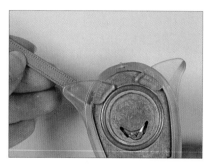

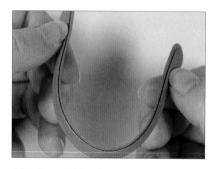

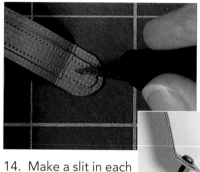

12. Use the corner-rounding punch to round the ends of the strip.

13. Cut a 15 x 1cm (6 x ½in) strip of brown card. Round the corners and stick the narrower strip to it with clear adhesive. Bend the strips as shown as you glue them so that they form a curved handle shape.

14. Make a slit in each end of the handle and push a brad through each of the slits (see inset).

15. Make two slits in the top of the bag, push the brads through and open them up to secure the handle to the bag.

16. Fold the bag along the score lines. Remove the backing from the tape on the lower flaps and stick them to the base as shown.

17. Remove the backing from the tape on the side flaps and fold the bag together.

18. Remove the backing from one side of the magnet and attach it to the middle front of the bag from the inside.

19. Place the other side of the magnet where it is attracted (see inset), then remove the backing and close the bag to attach the flap to the magnet.

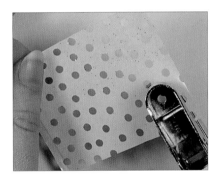

Tip

Use an eyelet-setting punch rather than small hole punches to create holes for backgrounds and borders. These are especially useful if your punch will not reach where you want the hole.

20. Cut a piece of double-sided punch tape and use the medium hole pliers punch to punch holes all over the piece as shown.

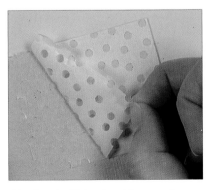

21. Peel off the backing and stick the punched tape to green card, then peel off the other side of the backing.

22. Sprinkle green glitter over the sticky area, then use the large five-petalled flower punch to punch out a flower.

23. Cut a piece of double-sided punch tape and stick it to pink card. Punch out a flower using the large daisy punch.

24. Peel off the backing and stick one of the scrap pieces of medium daisy backing (from step 8) to the centre of the flower.

25. Sprinkle the flower with dark pink glitter, then remove the mask of backing paper.

26. Sprinkle the flower centre with pink glitter and then use a 3D foam pad to attach the flower to the large green flower. Gently bend the petals of the daisy up to give a three-dimensional effect.

27. Punch an eight-pointed star from brown card, then use a glue pen on each point and sprinkle dark bronze glitter on the star.

28. Punch a tiny flower from glitter card with the flower pliers punch and stick it in the centre of the star. Fold the points of the star in slightly.

29. Attach the star to the flower with 3D foam pads, then attach the flower to the bag with some more 3D foam pads.

Tip

You can use the perforating tool to give the flap of the bag a stitched effect to match the strap.

Opposite

Present your gifts in style with this gorgeous girly gift bag, complete with glittery punched flowers.

Vary the colour, size and shape of your handbag template to create a whole boutique full of classy gift bags! Any flower punches can be used to create the embellishments; just experiment, glittering and layering those you have.

The templates for the green and brown bags shown here are on pages 78–79.

The pink bag is simply a larger version of the Glitzy Gift Bag; so enlarge the template on page 26 by 225 per cent on a photocopier.

Medallion-punched Box

Corner punches are designed to be used to punch a decorative corner on your greetings cards or scrapbook pages. In this project, however, I have used corner punches as the basis for an elaborately folded gift box decoration. The result may look complicated and time-consuming, but the technique is very simple because the filigree corner design does all the hard work for you.

This technique is a passage of discovery as it is difficult to tell from the punch image what the finished medallion will look like, but this is all part of the magic of medallion punching!

You will need

- Craft punches: scalloped border, small daisy, filigree corner, edging corner and large daisy
- Craft knife, cutting mat and ruler
- Ball-tipped stylus
- HB pencil
- 3D foam pads and double-sided tape
- Craft jewels
- Pink and rose glitter and glue pen
- Dark pink card 19.5 x 19.5cm (7¾ x 7¾in)
- Light pink card 14.7 x 14.7cm (5¾ x 5¾in)
- Sheets of card: silver, light pink, dark pink, dotted and double-sided with pattern
- Clear adhesive

1. Make pencil marks 6.5cm (2½in) in from each corner of the dark pink card, then use a ruler and the ball-tipped stylus to score between the lines to split the card into nine squares.

2. Use a craft knife to cut along four of the score lines to form flaps as shown.

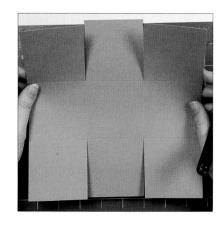

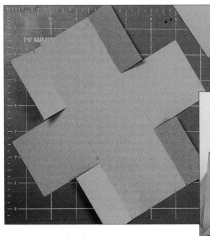

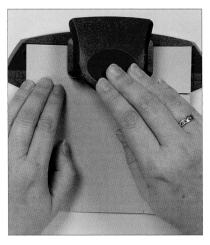

4. Run double-sided tape along the tabs and fold in along the score lines.

3. Form tabs by cutting across the flaps, roughly halfway down.

5. Remove the backing from the tape and assemble the bottom of the box.

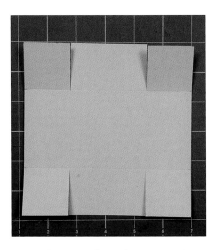

6. Make pencil marks 4cm (1½in) in from each corner of the light pink card, score between the lines and cut down the score lines to form flaps.

7. Put the cut light pink card in the scalloped border punch, making sure it is central, then punch the design out.

8. Move the card along so the silver design printed on the punch can be seen through the hole you have just punched. Punch the design out.

9. Punch the design along all the edges, then cut across the corner flaps with a knife as shown to make tabs.

10. Run double-sided tape down the corner tabs, remove the backing and fold the sides in to make the lid of the box.

11. Use the small daisy punch to punch out a daisy from dark pink card. Place a craft jewel in the centre, bend the petals in and attach it to the side of the lid with a dab of clear adhesive.

12. Repeat on the other three sides, place the lid on the box and then put it safely to one side.

13. Cut a square of dark pink card 6.5 x 6.5cm (2½ x 2½in) and use the filigree corner punch to punch each corner in turn.

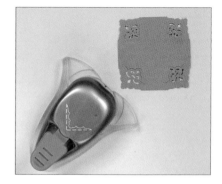

14. Use the edging corner punch to give the square decorative corners.

15. Using the punched design as a guide, score a line across the two sides of the corner.

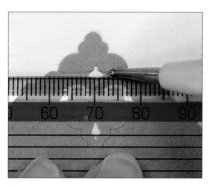

16. Make a second score line above the first.

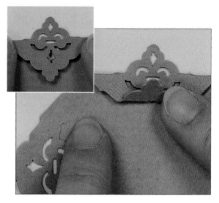

17. Fold in along the first score line, allowing the filigree design to remain unfolded as shown in the inset, then fold up along the second score line.

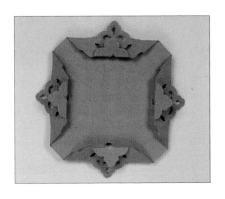

18. Repeat the folding on the other three sides.

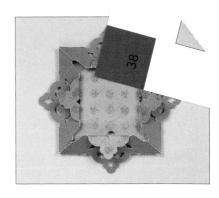

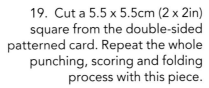

19. Cut a 5.5 x 5.5cm (2 x 2in) square from the double-sided patterned card. Repeat the whole punching, scoring and folding process with this piece.

20. Decorate the edges of both folded squares using a glue pen and glitter: pink on the darker card, rose on the double-sided card.

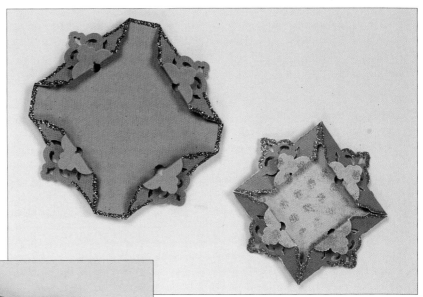

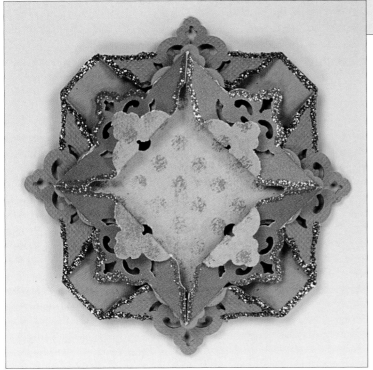

21. Put 3D foam pads on the back of the smaller folded square and mount it in the middle of the larger motif at the angle shown.

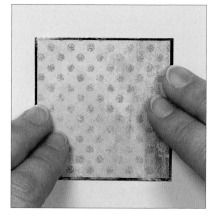

22. Punch a large daisy from light pink card and a small daisy from dark pink card. Add a craft jewel to the centre of the small daisy, then mount the smaller daisy on the larger with a 3D foam pad.

23. Use 3D foam pads to mount the flower on the folded squares and add craft jewels to each of the large flower's petals.

24. Cut a 5.5 x 5.5cm (2 x 2in) square of dotted card and attach it to a slightly larger square of silver card with double-sided tape.

25. Mount the folded squares on to the dotted square using 3D foam pads, then use double-sided tape to mount the decoration on the lid of the box.

This pretty gift box looks very complicated, but the technique is simple to master and will have the recipient wondering how you did it!

Only two different corner punches have been used to create all these variations. There are literally hundreds of medallion designs that can be created by simply stacking more squares or turning over or rotating the squares in different combinations.

...are my favourite flowers so when I saw this orchid punch I knew it was coming home with me! This punch is designed to be used to construct a three-dimensional orchid, but several different flower types are available as punches. The orchids made in this project can be used to create mini plants or as super embellishments for your cards.

You will need

- Craft punches: orchid, oval and small circle 1.6cm (⅝in)
- Craft knife, cutting mat, ruler and scissors
- Ball-tipped stylus
- Clear adhesive and tweezers
- Artist's chalks: pink, green and yellow
- Fine pink felt-tip pen
- Double-sided tape
- 16cm (6¼in) of high-gauge wire and 12cm (4¾in) of low-gauge wire
- Mini flowerpot and air-drying clay
- Modelling lichen
- Sheets of card: white and green

1. Use the orchid punch twice (see inset) and gather together these pieces.

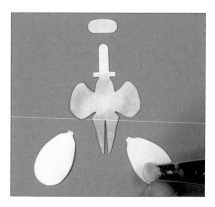

2. Chalk the stamen yellow, the lower petals slightly green and the inner petals pink.

3. Use a fine pink felt-tip pen to detail the inner petals and the stamen as shown.

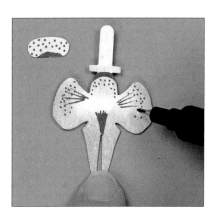

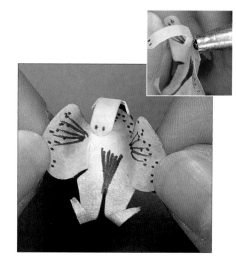

4. Use your fingers to fold the inner petals up as shown. Add a touch of chalk and pen to detail the parts that curl over, then add a dot of clear adhesive to the tabs (see inset).

5. Close the outer petals to glue them to the tabs, then fold the stamen, add a dab of clear adhesive and use tweezers to place it in the centre.

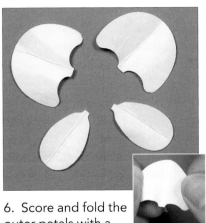

6. Score and fold the outer petals with a ruler and ball-tipped stylus, then use your fingers (see inset) to give each petal a slight curve.

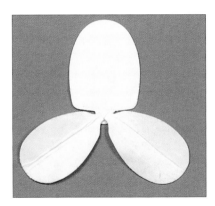

7. Add a dab of glue to the tab of the central petal and place the shaped lower petals on the tab.

8. Add glue to the tabs of the shaped upper petals and attach them at the same point.

9. Glue the inside of the orchid to the outer petals, then make a second orchid in the same way.

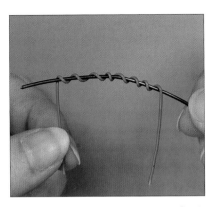

10. Wrap the high-gauge (softer) wire around the low-gauge (firmer) wire, leaving approximately 3cm (1¼in) at both ends unwrapped.

11. Put a strip of double-sided tape on the edge of the white card, then use the circle punch to punch through twice.

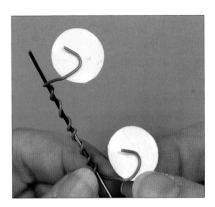

12. Bend both loose ends of the high-gauge wire into curves, then remove the backing from the white circles and place them on the wire.

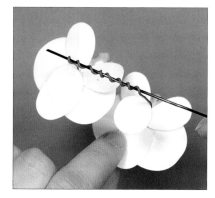

13. Stick the backs of the orchid flowers to the sticky circles.

14. Fill a mini flowerpot with air-drying clay and push the wire flower stem into the clay.

15. Punch three ovals from green card with the oval punch, then fold them in half and trim either side of the fold lines to make leaf shapes.

16. Use your fingers to shape the leaves and glue them together as shown.

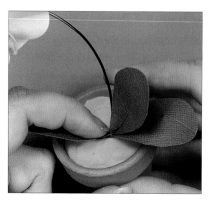

17. Push the leaves into the air-drying clay.

18. Cover the air-drying clay with modelling lichen to finish.

Opposite
This orchid will flower continually, needs no care or attention and certainly no watering!

Regular flower punches can also be used to create three-dimensional plants and flowers. The cactus is made from a large daisy curled into a ball with tiny daisy flowers and fern fronds making the spikes. Each of the daffodil flowers is made up of a small daisy with its petals folded to form the trumpet, mounted on to a five-pointed flower.

Opposite
Use a flowerpot punch to create mini flowers for your greetings cards.The geranium is made up of layers of punched stamen shapes with tiny daisies on each end.

Magic Box

To get the very most from my craft punches I like to use them in as many ways as possible. What you can create with craft punches is only limited by your own imagination, and this project proves the point, using regular punches to create three-dimensional figures. The basic cone is simply half of a punched circle, the face an egg shape, and the hair is made from a punched flower shape.

You will need

- Craft punches: star pliers, buttonhole pliers, very large circle 7.5cm (3in), medium squeeze circle 2.5cm (1in), small circle 1.6cm (⅝in), large daisy, egg, eight-pointed flower, flowerpot, medium daisy, spiral, oval

- Craft knife, cutting mat and ruler

- Clear adhesive

- Box blank

- Glitter and glue pen

- Pencil

- Foam squares, double-sided tape and tweezers

- Green and white chalk

- Orange acrylic paint and brush

- Sheets of card: green, dark green, purple, lilac, black, orange

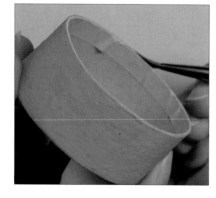

1. Paint the bottom part of the box blank with orange paint and leave it to dry.

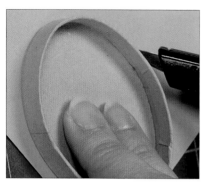

2. Glue the lid to green card and use a craft knife to cut around it.

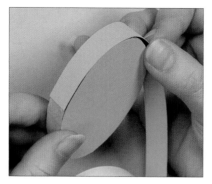

3. Cut a strip of green card the same width as the height of the lid. Run double-sided tape down the strip, remove the backing and attach it to the side of the lid.

4. Use the star pliers punch to punch eighteen small stars from dark green card. Use clear adhesive to attach them around the side of the lid.

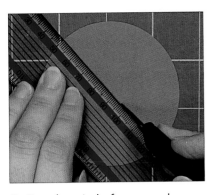

5. Punch a circle from purple card with the 7.5cm (3in) punch. Cut it in half with a craft knife and ruler.

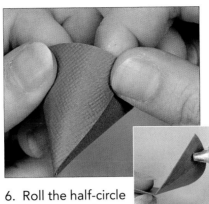

6. Roll the half-circle into a cone and secure with clear adhesive (see inset).

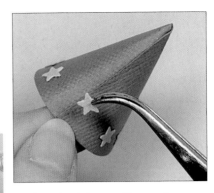

7. Punch eight small stars from lilac card with the small star pliers punch. Glue them to the bottom of the cone.

8. Cut a 4.5 x 0.5cm (1¾ x ¼in) strip of purple card and punch out a large daisy from green card. Trim the ends of two petals and glue one to each end of the strip.

9. Punch an oval from black card and draw a wavy line around the edge with a glue pen. Sprinkle with glitter, then gently curve it with your fingers.

10. Glue the arms on to the cone with a dab of glue in the middle of the purple strip, then glue on the oval as a cape.

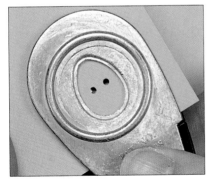

11. Use the buttonhole pliers punch to make two holes in green card, then use the egg-shaped punch to punch out the witch's face.

12. Glue a scrap of black card behind the eyes, add two dabs of green chalk on the witch's cheeks and draw on a smile with a pencil.

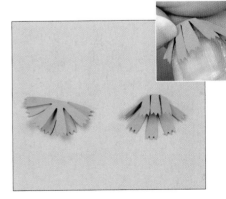

13. Use the eight-pointed flower punch to punch two flowers from dark green card. Fold one in half and wrap the other around your thumb (see inset).

14. Glue the thumb-folded shape to the witch's forehead and stick the other piece on the back of the head with clear adhesive (see inset).

15. Punch a small circle from black card and make a small slit, then punch a medium black circle with the squeeze punch. Cut it in half and make a cone. Glue the cone to the small circle. Use the star pliers punch to punch an orange star and glue it on.

16. Add glue to the witch's hair, push it into the slot of the hat. Glue the witch's head to the body.

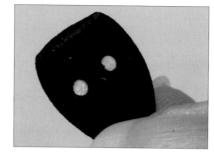

17. Fold a piece of black card in half and place it in the flowerpot punch, making sure the fold is aligned with the bottom of the pot. Punch out the shape shown.

18. Make the cat's head by punching eyes with the buttonhole punch, then the face with the egg punch. Glue a scrap of green card behind the eyes and fold the top over.

19. Punch a medium daisy from black card, and cut two petals off as a single piece. Crease them as shown to make ears for the cat.

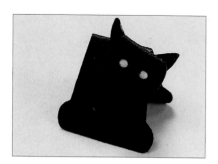

20. Glue the ears to the back of the cat's head, then mount the head on the body with a foam square.

21. Punch a tail from black card with the spiral punch and glue it to the body. Use a little white chalk to give the cat whiskers.

22. Glue the witch and her cat to the top of the box to finish.

If you want to use your witch to decorate a card or gift tag simply squash the main body cone so that it is flatter, then stick it to the front of the card.

Create charming flower fairies by adapting the basic technique. Follow the directions to make the witch's body, arms and head, then add punched flowers as layered skirts and for hats.

The neat fairy hair is made from a flowerpot punched shape, with the rim folded to make the fringe. The fairy wings are made from two leaf shapes.

Gift Wallet

When giving a gift of money or a voucher it is often nice to make an extra special effort to present the gift in a wallet type card. With all the hundreds of flower punches available, it is sometimes difficult to create punched cards for a male recipient. This gift wallet uses a more masculine colour palette and punched elements that are not too flowery! A humble office hole punch is used to great effect in this project to create a funky border strip.

You will need

- Craft punches: large hole pliers 7mm (¼in), medium hole pliers 3mm (⅛in), small hole pliers 1.5mm (¹⁄₁₆in), tag, double square, small circle, corner-rounding
- Craft knife and cutting mat
- Clear adhesive
- Pencil and ruler
- Decorative brad
- Magnets
- 3D foam pads and double-sided tape
- Black card 30 x 15cm (12 x 6in)
- Sheets of card: patterned red, green, blue, striped green, striped blue and red, floral red
- 20cm (8in) ribbon
- 35cm (14in) cord
- Large and small eyelets, eyelet setting tool and hammer

1. Fold the black card in half and open it up, then score a line 10.5cm (4¼in) from the top across the whole piece.

2. Cut away the rectangle on the bottom left made by the fold and score line.

3. Run thin strips of double-sided tape up both sides of the remaining rectangle on the lower right, remove the backing and fold the rectangle up to form a pocket (see inset).

4. Close the wallet and then cut a 15 x 3.5cm (6 x 1½in) strip of patterned red card. Use double-sided tape to attach the strip to the front of the card.

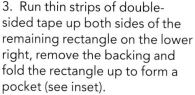

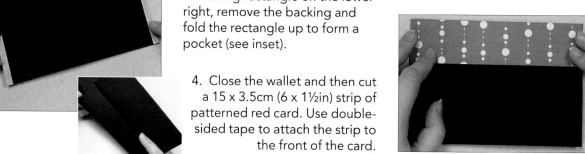

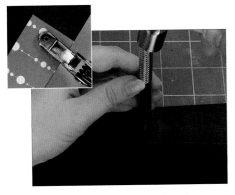

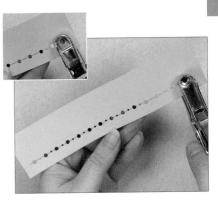

5. Use the medium hole pliers punch to punch a hole centrally in both ends of the strip, 1cm (½in) in from the edge (see inset). Set a small eyelet in each hole.

6. Cut a strip of green card at least 16cm (6¼in) long and draw a line on the back. Make a pencil mark every 0.5cm (¼in) along this line.

7. Punch every second hole with the medium hole pliers punch (see inset), then punch the remaining holes with the small hole pliers punch.

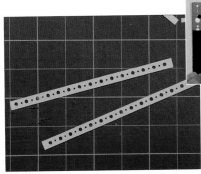

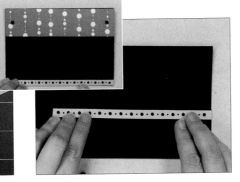

8. Trim the strip down to 15cm x 1cm (6 x ½in), then make another in the same way.

9. Use clear adhesive to stick one of the strips to the bottom of the front and the other to the top of the inside pocket.

10. Punch a tag from blue card, then punch a hole in the top with the large pliers punch and set a large eyelet in the hole.

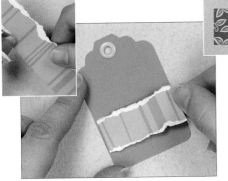

11. Cut a 3cm (1¼in) wide strip of striped green paper and tear the edges. Cut it down to the width of the tag and attach it with double-sided tape.

12. Use the larger square of the double punch to punch out a square from striped red and blue card, and the smaller square to punch a floral square (see inset). Cut the larger square in half and mount the red part on the smaller square using 3D foam pads.

13. Wrap the ribbon around the square and tie it in a knot to form a gift box. Attach the gift box to the tag with 3D foam pads (see inset).

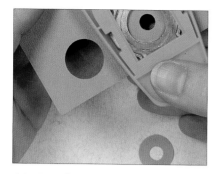

14. Punch two holes in blue card with the large hole pliers punch, then use the small circle punch to punch out washer shapes.

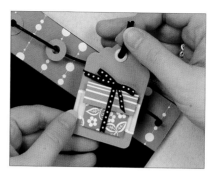

15. Thread cord through the eyelets of the wallet so both loose ends are at the front. Slip the two washers on to the left end, then take both ends through the tag's eyelet and tie a knot.

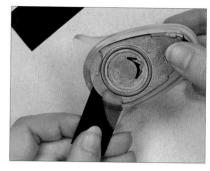

16. Cut two strips of black card, one 5.5 x 2.5cm (2¼ x 1in) and one 5.2 x 2cm (2 x ¾in). Use the corner-rounding punch to round one end of each.

17. Cut a small slit near the rounded end of the narrower strip and insert a decorative brad.

18. Open the brad up and attach a magnet over it, and then glue the wider piece of card to the back (see inset) to make a fastener.

19. Fold the fastener around the wallet, and glue it to the back of the wallet.

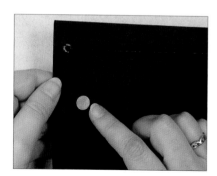

20. Attach the other half of the magnet to the inside front of the wallet. Make sure that the wallet closes securely.

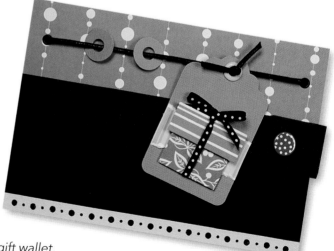

The finished gift wallet.

For a variation on the project, create a simple pouch with a pull-out sheet complete with a small gift pocket inside. Add a punched tag for decoration.

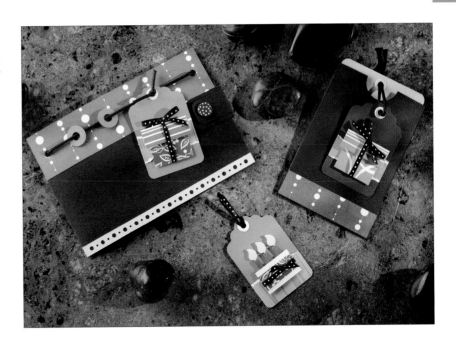

It is time to get all girly again! These gift wallets are created in a pink and zebra stripe colour scheme for a really sassy look.

Floral Tin

Altered art is a hot new trend in crafting and this project uses a regular paint tin as the basis for an unusual gift box. Many different shapes and sizes of tin, specifically designed to be decorated, are available at craft stores.

This project uses a border punch to create a continuous border design that gives a pretty, lacy look, ideal for combining with flower punches and patterned papers.

You will need

- Craft punches: giant daisy, large circle 2.7cm (1¹⁄₁₆in in), very large circle 5cm (2in), small hole pliers 3mm (⅛in), large hole pliers 7mm (¼in), flourish border, slot pliers, tag

- Craft knife, cutting mat and ruler

- Sheets of card: peach, red, plain green, striped, green floral and multicoloured floral

- Circle cutter and pencil

- Cotton wool and tweezers

- 3D foam pads and double-sided tape

- 1m (39½in) ribbon

- Red, green and orange chalk

- Blank 1 litre paint tin

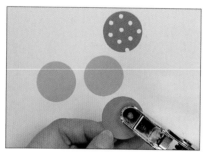

1. Punch two daisies from peach card, using the giant daisy punch. Bend the petals slightly.

2. Punch two circles from green card with the large circle punch, then run double-sided tape on the back of red card and punch two circles from the card. Punch holes in the red circles with the small hole pliers punch.

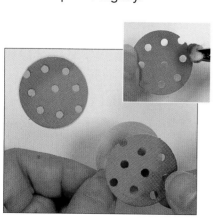

3. Chalk a red crescent on the red circles with chalk (see inset). Remove the backing from the red circles and stick them on to the green circles.

4. Attach the circles to the flowers with 3D foam pads, and add 3D foam pads to the back of the flowers.

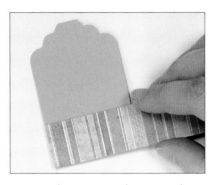

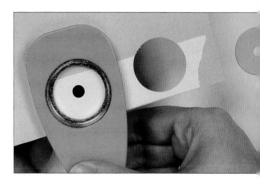

5. Use the tag punch to punch a tag from green card, then stick a 2 x 8cm (¾ x 3¼in) strip of striped card to the tag with double-sided tape.

6. Carefully trim the strip round the shape of the tag, then chalk round the edges with green chalk.

7. Run double-sided tape along the peach card and punch two holes with the large hole pliers punch. Then use the large circle punch to punch rings around the holes.

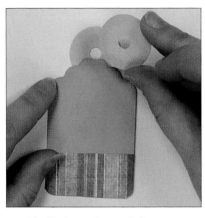

8. Chalk the edges of the rings with orange chalk and remove the backing. Put one ring on the back and one on the front of the tag as shown.

9. Cut a 36.5 x 7.5cm (14½ x 3in) strip of floral paper and wrap it round the tin, using double-sided tape to secure it.

10. Cut a strip of green floral card 36.5 x 7.5cm (14 x 3in) and remove the guides from the flourish border punch (see inset). Punch the design, then move the punch along so it overlaps the end of the previous flourish.

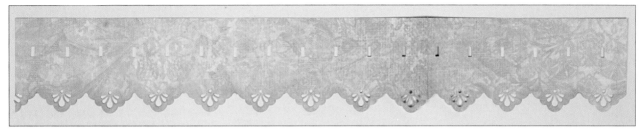

11. Continue along the strip until the whole edge has been punched. Carefully mark the back at 2cm (1in) intervals and use the slot pliers punch to punch slots at each point. Finally, chalk the border with green chalk.

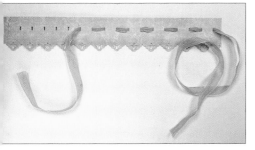

12. Starting from the middle of the strip, thread a ribbon through the slots, taking the ribbon down one hole and up the next.

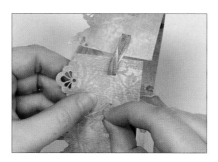

13. When you reach the end, bend the strip in a loop and thread the ribbon into the slot at the other end.

14. Thread the rest of the slots loosely.

15. Run double-sided tape along the ends of the card, slip it over the top of the tin, remove the backing, gently tighten the ribbon and stick the ends of the strip together.

16. Thread the tag on to the ribbon and tie the ribbon in a bow.

17. Use a circle cutter to cut a 9cm (3½in) circle from striped card, chalk the edges orange and use double-sided tape to stick it to the lid of the tin.

18. Punch a green circle with the very large circle punch, chalk the edges with green chalk and mount in the centre of the lid with 3D foam pads.

19. Remove the backing from the flowers and place one on the lid and one on the tag.

The finished floral tin.

This tin would be ideal for packing with bath salts or homemade biscuits for a special gift.

These pretty pink and green shades create a funky look for the covered tins. Large, bold punch shapes such as the big tag and daisy work well with the bold patterned papers. The smallest tin is actually a green tea tub covered to match the others – a cheaper, recycled alternative!

Opposite
Large 2½ litre paint tins look great covered with bold patterned papers. This tin would be ideal for storing your craft materials.

Decorated Notebook

This pretty notebook would make a lovely gift, or you could use it as a special photograph album or scrapbook. The technique uses a foam stamp to create a background image for the punched blossom. The punched flowers are stuck down flat as this is more practical for a notebook, but this design could easily be adapted for cards and the blossom fixed with 3D foam pads for added dimension.

You will need

- Craft punches: large blossom, small blossom, stamen, large leaf, small leaf and large pliers punch 7mm (¼in)
- Craft knife, cutting mat and ruler
- Pencil
- Sheets of card: pink patterned, pink dotted, brown, pale pink
- Sheets of plain white paper
- Brown and red ink and ink applicator
- Large swirl foam stamp
- Sheets of mountboard: 19 x 16cm (7½ x 6¼in), 0.9 x 16cm (½ x 6¼in), 2.9 x 16cm (1 x 6¼in) and 15.9 x 16cm (6³⁄₁₆ x 6¼in)
- 3D foam pads and double-sided tape
- Red eyelets, eyelet setting tool and hammer
- 75cm (30in) ribbon
- Clear adhesive

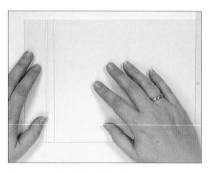

1. Use double-sided tape to attach the 19 x 16cm (7½ x 6¼in), 0.9 x 16cm (½ x 6¼in) and 2.9 x 16cm (1 x 6¼in) pieces of mountboard to the back of your pink patterned card as shown. Leave a gap of 1.5mm (¹⁄₁₆in) between each piece.

2. Cut away the excess card using a craft knife. Make two pencil marks on the 2.9 x 16cm (1 x 6¼in) piece, 3.5cm (1½in) from the top and the bottom respectively. Make two pencil marks on the 19 x 16cm (7½ x 6¼in) piece parallel with the other marks, and 1.5cm (¾in) in from the left edge as shown.

3. Use the eyelet setting tool to punch holes at each mark.

4. Turn the cover over and set an eyelet in each hole. This completes the back cover.

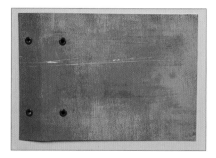

5. Ink the edge of the cover with red ink and put it to one side to dry thoroughly.

6. Glue the last piece of mountboard to brown card and cut round it, leaving 3cm (1¼in) of brown paper on the left-hand side as shown to make the front cover.

7. Make two holes in the brown card with the large pliers punch, one 3.5cm (1½in) from the top and one 3.5cm (1½in) from the bottom. Ink the edge of the mountboard with brown ink and allow to dry.

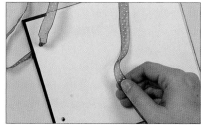

8. Cut forty to fifty pieces of white paper to 14.8 x 18cm (5¾ x 7in), and make holes 3.4cm (1⁷⁄₁₆in) from the top and 3.4cm (1⁷⁄₁₆in) from the bottom. The holes should be 1cm (½in) from the left edge. Place the paper on the front cover and thread the ribbon through the hole at the top.

9. Pull the ribbon through the top eyelet on the back cover.

10. Repeat this with the lower eyelet, then turn the book over and fold the back cover flap round to the front to form a spine for the book.

11. Thread the ribbon through the holes in the flap and tie it in a bow.

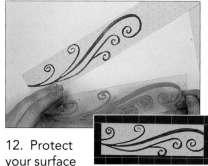

12. Protect your surface with scrap paper, then ink the large swirl stamp with brown ink and stamp a 4.5 x 30cm (1¾ x 12in) piece of dotted paper. Cut the strip to 16cm (6¼in), cutting across the design (see inset).

13. Attach some pink patterned card to mountboard, cut it to 5 x 16cm (2 x 6¼in) and ink the edges red. Use double-sided tape to attach the swirl-stamped paper to this piece.

14. Use the large blossom punch to punch three pink and three pale pink blossoms, and the small blossom punch to punch one pink and one pale pink blossom.

15. Punch two brown, four pink and two pale pink stamens with the stamen punch.

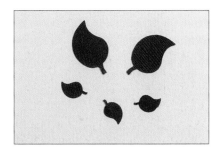

16. Punch two large and three small leaves from brown paper using the large and small leaf punches.

17. Use clear adhesive to attach three of the pink stamens to the large pale pink blossoms, then glue the brown stamens to two of the large pink blossoms. Finally, glue one of the pale pink stamens to the remaining large pink blossom.

18. Trim the remaining stamens down to just three points, then glue the pale pink piece to the small pink blossom and the pink piece to the small pale pink blossom.

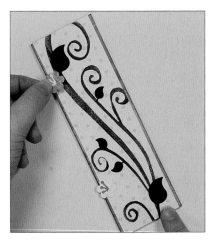

19. Glue the leaves and small blossoms on to the swirl-stamped panel as shown.

20. Glue the large blossoms on to the swirl-stamped panel to complete the decoration.

21. Attach the decoration to the right-hand side of the front cover with double-sided tape.

Opposite
This notebook features simple punching on a stamped background.

Alter the colour scheme to a vibrant black, orange and red to give your notebooks an oriental feel. For a quicker notebook, simply decorate the front of a ready-made book. Make a concertina notebook with one long folded piece of card for the pages, covered front and back with decorated mountboard squares and tied at either side.

Artist Trading Card

Artist trading cards are a huge new trend. Artists create mini artworks and swap them with others to build up a collection of art. Just stick to the size of 6.3 x 9cm (2½ x 3½in) and decorate the cards in your own artistic style. Make sure you sign and date your cards on the back.

You will need

- Craft punches: corner-rounding, diamond border, spiral, eight-pointed star, five-pointed star, large blossom, large retro flower

- Craft knife, cutting mat and ruler

- Pencil

- Sheets of card: white, yellow, green, pink and orange.

- Sheets of paper: yellow floral, pink, pink patterned, dotted

- Glue pen

- Yellow, orange and pink glitter

- 3D foam pads and double-sided tape

- Round and square craft jewels

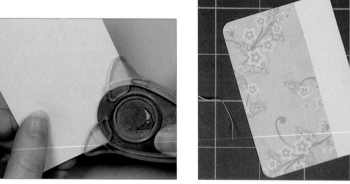

1. Cut a piece of white card 6.3 x 9cm (2½ x 3½in) and use the corner-rounding punch on each corner.

2. Use double-sided tape to secure a 5 x 9cm (2 x 3½in) piece of yellow floral paper to the card, just off-centre. Cut away the excess paper by trimming to the edge of the card from the back.

3. Use the diamond border punch to punch pink paper, then move the paper until the pattern on the punch can be seen through the holes. Punch the paper a second time to create a continuous pattern.

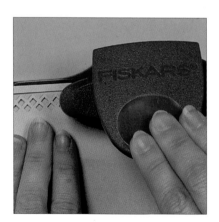

4. Trim the pattern into a thin strip slightly longer than 9cm (3½in), and glue it to the card.

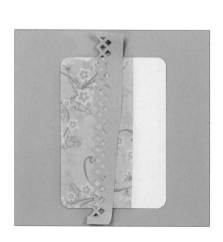

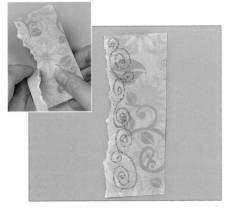

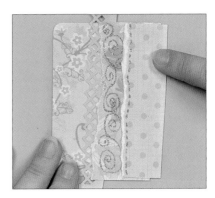

5. Tear a 9cm (3½in) strip from pink patterned paper (see inset). Use a glue pen and pink glitter to decorate it with a spiral design.

6. Attach the strip to the trading card with double-sided tape.

7. Tear a 9cm (3½in) strip from dotted paper, decorate with a glue pen and pink glitter. Attach it to the card with double-sided tape.

8. Turn the card over and use a craft knife to trim the excess paper away from the card.

9. Punch three spirals from yellow card, two eight-pointed stars from white card and one five-pointed star from green card.

10. Glue the spirals on to the front of the card as shown.

11. Glue the stars on to the front of the card as shown.

12. Use a craft knife to carefully trim away any parts of the stars and spirals that overlap the edge of the card.

13. Punch a large blossom from yellow card, an eight-pointed star from pink card and a large retro flower from orange card.

14. Draw a spiral design on the large retro flower with the glue pen and sprinkle orange glitter over it.

15. Use the glue pen to draw lines on the yellow blossom, add yellow glitter and mount on the flower using 3D foam pads.

16. Mount the pink eight-pointed star on the yellow blossom with a 3D foam pad.

17. Mount the flower on the card with 3D foam pads, then decorate the eight-pointed stars with round and square craft jewels.

The finished artist trading card.

An artist trading card reflects the artist's own style. For my cards I have used some of my favourite materials such as glitter and craft jewels.

Artists normally produce a series of cards in a very similar style to swap.

All of these cards use the same elements, punches, papers and embellishments, but are all subtly different.

Artist trading cards also make great toppers for greetings cards.

Framed Collage

Punched shapes can be used as abstract design elements, as shown by this framed collage picture. The key to the success of this project lies in the choice of materials. Pick a range of papers and embellishments that match well, but also have texture and interest. When you have chosen, stick to those materials and repeat their use, to get a coordinated look.

You will need

- Craft punches: double square punch, leaf, stamp, buttonhole pliers, large blossom
- Craft knife, cutting mat and ruler
- Sheets of card: plain beige, plain brown, patterned brown, patterned beige, red glitter, embossed white, plain cream and dotted
- Stapler and red staples
- Needle and peach embroidery thread
- Four beads and a two-hole button
- 3D foam pads and double-sided tape
- Perforating tool
- Box frame

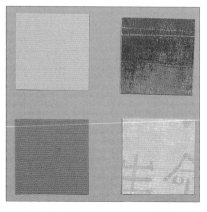

1. Use the larger square of the double square punch to punch four squares: one plain beige, one plain brown, one patterned brown and one patterned beige.

2. Tear the plain brown square in half.

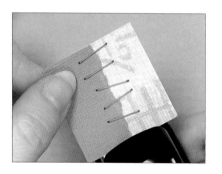

3. Using red staples, staple half of the torn square to the patterned beige square.

4. Use the leaf punch to punch a leaf shape from red glitter card.

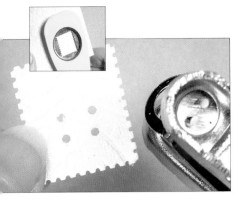

5. Use the stamp punch to punch a stamp from embossed card (see inset), then punch four holes in the stamp with the buttonhole pliers punch as shown.

6. Thread a needle with three strands of peach embroidery thread. Place the leaf on the stamp and bring the needle through the top right hole and down through the bottom left.

7. Take the thread up through the bottom right hole and down the top left hole to make a cross stitch to hold the leaf in place.

8. Bring the needle up through the top right hole and thread a bead on to it.

9. Complete another cross stitch to hold the bead in place, then trim the thread and use two 3D foam pads to secure the thread at the back (see inset).

10. Remove the backing from the 3D foam pads and place the stamp on to the stapled piece you prepared earlier.

11. Tear a third from the patterned brown square (see inset), then stick the larger part to the plain beige square using double-sided tape.

12. Use the buttonhole pliers punch as shown to punch four holes in the prepared piece.

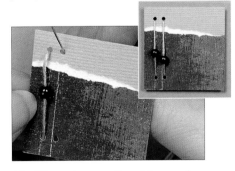

13. Thread a needle with peach embroidery thread, bring it up through the top left hole and thread on a bead. Take the needle down the bottom left hole and then repeat in the other holes (see inset). Secure on the back with 3D foam pads.

14. Punch a large blossom from dotted card, then punch a pair of holes with the buttonhole pliers punch.

15. Thread a needle with peach thread and secure a button to the blossom (see inset), then bring the thread up through the left hole, thread on a bead and take the needle down through the right hole. Trim and secure the thread with 3D foam pads on the back.

16. Remove the backing from the 3D foam pads and place the blossom on the stitched piece.

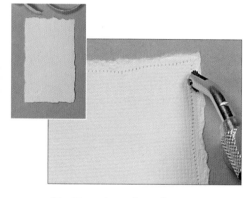

17. Tear the edges from a 7 x 10cm (2¾ x 4in) piece of plain cream card (see inset), then give the piece a perforated border with the perforating tool.

19. Place the piece in the frame to finish.

18. Mount the two prepared pieces on the torn card with 3D foam pads.

Opposite
This simple collage is quick to make and any punches that you already have can be used to make a variation.

Opposite
Using the same technique, make more squares to create a larger collage; or mount a single square on a card blank for an attractive all-purpose greetings card.

Punched tag shapes are used as the basis for these collage pictures. Experiment with other punched shapes for different looks and coordinate the colours of your papers and embellishments to your home decor to create unique, personalised wall art.

Templates

The templates shown here are for the gift bags shown on pages 32 and 33. All of these templates are reproduced here at half of the actual size. You will need to enlarge each by 200 per cent on a photocopier.

The template for the lime green bag on page 32.

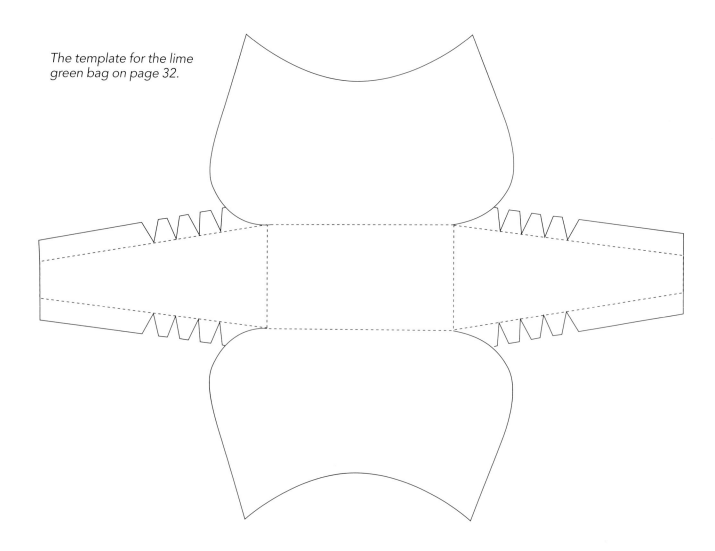

*The template for the small
brown bag on page 33.*

*The template for the large
brown bag on page 33.*

Index